Claudette Milner

,

Forgiven of Our Transgr

By

Claudette Milner

Forgiven of Our Transgressions: Nancy Deming, Faith

Acknowledgement

To God be the Glory
It is my Faith that has kept me and my Praise that has sustained me.
The answer to struggle is Praise
The answer to success is Praise
Please be a blessing to someone during the Thanksgiving holidays and the celebration of the birth of our Savior.

Claudette Milner

Dedication

Forgiven of Our Trespasses: Nancy Deming, Faith is dedicated to my family, prayer warriors, and friends that have walked this journey with me.

Forgiven of Our Transgressions: Nancy Deming, Faith

Table of Contents

Prologue	*Page*	*5*
Fatherhood	*Page*	*13*
Love	*Page*	*22*
Family	*Page*	*30*
About the Series	*Page*	*40*
About the Author	*Page*	*41*
Contact Us	*Page*	*42*

Claudette Milner
,

Prologue
Faith
1st Peter 1: 8-9

[8] Though you have not seen him, you love him; and even though you do not see him now, you believe in him and are filled with an inexpressible and glorious joy, [9] for you are receiving the end result of your faith, the salvation of your souls.

Theresa Deming was working a 36 hour shift. She had been working at Atlanta General Hospital for the last eight years. She had returned from Texas after Nancy was born. She had been working in the emergency room at Texas General when she met Sgt. Donald Miller. He was stationed at Fort Hood near Killeen TX. They met when he came into the emergency to have his hand examined. He was scheduled to be deployed but he had not been given his instructions. He had served two tours of duty already. This would be his last. They were getting to know each other when she found out she was pregnant. She knew he was not in it for the long haul. When he was deployed, he could not maintain contact with her. His location was concealed. He offered to put Nancy on his insurance after the DNA test. She took the test but declined his help. After Nancy was born, she moved back to Atlanta. She added his name to the birth certificate incase anything ever happened to her. The last time she saw Donald Miller was before he was deployed. He had enlisted for another tour of duty. He wanted to see Nancy before he left. He came to Atlanta and met his daughter. He took a couple of pictures. His parents had recently moved from Colorado to Tacoma Washington. Colorado was his last listed address for him. They were no longer at that address. When she became ill. she tried to reach them, but she had no idea how to locate them. All she knew was that he grew up in Colorado. She knew she needed to get in her safety deposit box and pull out the birth certificate and the DNA test so that Donald could be located. A friend at her church was keeping Nancy for her. She was one of the mother's of the church. When Theresa came into work that next day, she tested positive for Covid 19. After a month she knew she would not make it. Her lockbox key was in her personal items. They would let her talk to Nancy for ten minutes on the phone each night. Mother Florence tried to prepare Nancy for her death. She would pray every night with Nancy then it was over.

At 6:00 AM Mother Florence received the call that Theresa Deming had passed She called Reverend Cook and the funeral home. Due to Covid guidelines there was no service. Theresa's personal affects were turned over to Mother Florence. She put them away for Nancy.

Nancy had been praying nightly for her mother. Each time she talked to her she slowly began to lose faith. She knew she had a father named Donald Miller. When he visited one day, he wore a military uniform. He told her he was born in Colorado, but his parents were now in Washington. He had not been to see them since they moved. He did not have their address, but he would give them her address. She wrote it down and he put it in his pocket. He had advised Theresa that he would put Nancy on his insurance when he returned stateside. He wanted to do things right. He promised Nancy he would come see her when he returned. He hugged her before he left. She knew her mother had a safety deposit box, but she did not have a key. She stayed with Mother Florence until she became ill. There was no place for her to go. They had to put her in foster care. She stayed with Roberta Heming and was enrolled in Cromley Elementary. Nancy had always been a good student. Her mother valued education. Although she worked long hours, she had made sure that she supported her dream of being an astronaut. Roberta talked with Nancy many times. She took her to church with her. Nancy told her what she knew about her father. She gave the information to the social worker.

They were sending for the birth certificate in hopes that they could find her father. She was born in Texas. For the military they also needed a DNA test. Nancy cried a lot. Mrs. Roberta kept her busy talking about her dreams. She gave her extra assignments at night. She had two older foster children with homework every night. She would copy their homework and give it to Nancy to complete. She had the social worker pull her academic records. Nancy was in the system. She had watched children fall through the cracks when they entered foster care. She was not going to let this little girl that was passionate about learning become invisible.

Nancy came home one day excited. She had heard in the hallway that the school was taking a trip to Conoco. When she asked her teacher about signing up, she was told that only the STEM students could participate. She went home crying. When Mrs. Heming gave her, tonight's assignment she rejected it.

Nancy, "what's wrong? Are you feeling ok?"

Nancy replied. "I do all this extra work and they still won't let me in the class with the smart kids. My mother always said never let anyone tell me I'm not good enough. They said I can not go on the field trip with the STEM students.

They didn't tell me why I'm not as smart as the others." Nancy began crying.

Roberta gathered her into her arms and held her then she spoke.

"Nancy, you were created by God to accomplish great things."

Nancy replied. "It doesn't matter if they shut the door on my dreams."

"Nancy, you have to believe it. You have to believe in yourself then you have to trust God. Make them tell you why you can't go. Fight for your right to go."

When Nancy got to school,

Nancy walked to Ms. Steele's desk.

"Ms. Steele, I need to see the counselor.

"Nancy, are you ok? Is there something I can do for you?"

"Yes, I want to know why I cannot go on the field trip with the smart kids. I want to be an astronaut, so I want to visit Conoco Aeronautics. I am finish with my work for the week. My foster mother said I have to prove that I am smart enough. Here is my folder of extra work Mrs. Roberta makes me complete every night. Can I go see my counselor?"

"Nancy, can I look at them first then you can go see Mrs. Simpson at the end of the period."

Ms. Steele ate lunch in her room so she could review the paperwork. She looked at her 3rd grade test scores. She expected to see Needs Improvement, but she saw distinguished in every area. She also noticed that her file was flagged. She looked up the code. It read Foster Care – No Permanent Address. Assign to General Education. She knew something was wrong. She decided that Nancy deserved answers. Since Nancy was finished with her assignment, she took her to the office to meet the new counselor Mrs. Simpson.

Ms. Steele went in to see Mrs. Simpson first. She explained the situation to her. After her discussion with Nancy she carried her folder to the principal. Mrs. Steele pulled the folders of the transfer children that were flagged in the system. She saw that they had denied access to the AP classes to at least 10 students because their address was either temporary or located in the poverty district. The first step was to open the field trip to all interested students in the 4th grade and up. Then they would place them equally with the other students beginning next year.

When Nancy came home from Conoco, she was excited. She met three female aeronautical engineers. She explained to Mrs., Roberta that there was a female engineer that looked just like her.

Claudette Milner

Roberta had just been notified that Nancy's father, Sgt Donald Miller, and her grandparents were in town to take custody of her. This young lady had trusted God and now she would be with her family. The one thing she was sure of was that God was directing her path. That night she gave Nancy the news.

The Miller's had to wait until all the paperwork was complete. The state had to file the paperwork to open the safety deposit box. In it was Nancy's birth certificate and her DNA test. The military requested a second test. Because Donald would be a single parent, he had to transfer custody to his parents. He took leave until the end of the semester then he would accompany Nancy to Washington. She had suffered enough grief. It was time he stepped up to take care of his daughter. His parents agreed to take custody until he retired during this final tour of duty. His father made sure he understood that he reared him to be a man. The family would support him, but they would not rear her for him.

Joseph spoke to him before he left to return home. "Donald, when Nancy was born you may have offered child support and insurance, but you refused to be her father. Her mother is dead. She has no other parent. God has expectations of you as a man and a parent. Do not break this little girl's heart again. One day you will understand that she is your greatest blessing. She is a part of you. I have always been proud of you for your service to this country. It is more important for me to be proud of you as a father. I love you Donald."

His father would no longer measure him by the number of medals and bars on his jacket. but he would measure hum by the love he showed for his child.

Claudette Milner

**Chapter 1
Fatherhood
Psalms 127:3**

3 Children are a gift from the Lord, they are a reward from him

Donald called Catherine. He had not thought about her since he received the news. He had met with Nancy with his parents several times during their visit while they waited for all the paperwork to be processed. He had driven them to the airport in the rental car. He was flying back to Texas in order to drive his car back. The Army Reserve base in Forest Park had handled all his paperwork. They were waiting on the final DNA anaylisis. He had seen Theresa's copy and knew that she was his daughter. He had six weeks until school was out. The military provided him temporary housing.

Catherine had been in his life for three years. She was the person he was with when he was back in the country. He never thought about making it a permanent relationship but it worked for now. The only thing that she knew was that he had returned to the states and that he was in Atlanta taking care of a family emergency. When she found out that his parents were joining him she asked did he need her to come and support him. At first he did not understand the question. How was she defining their relationship. They spent time together. Everything he knew about her was superficial. Things had always been that way between he and the women he dated. Of the three years he and Catherine were together he was on tour two of those years. He had been wounded. He had been afraid he would die in Iraq but he never shared his deamons with anyone. He couldn't. War does strange things to you. It produces nightmares. This last tour, for the first time, he began to pray. His father is a Baptist minister. He grew up in the church. He believed in God until he saw the devastation. The senseless murders of his bothers. These men were not co-workers they were family. They protected each other. Some were old and some young. Death did not respect age or experience. It just came. He questioned why God sent him to Iraq when there was a war being caried out in his home country. There was a war against crime, drugs, and the use of assault weapons. Murder was at a national high, senseless cop murders were looked at only a minute. Hate crimes came back with a not guilty verdict. Why did a God of mercy and compassion allow this to happen? He asked himself with Covid 19 and crime on the rise who was protecting his daughter. He began to pray for her that she remain safe until he returned home. She only had him to protect her. Theresa had born the responsibility of rearing their daughter since she was born. It was time to put in his retirement papers. He would transfer custody to his parents until retirement. He had reenlisted two times because the money was good. He was incharge of bomb detonation. He was not sure if he would be a contractor or work for law enforcement. What he now realized was that he had a child. He had to make his decisions carefully. His life was no longer his own. The . military gave him six weeks leave. He would remain in Texas until he retired.

He had no clue what to tell Catherine. He would visit Nancy as much as he could. He owed the military six more months overseas then he would return to regular duty.

Her phone rang. He almost hung up then she answered. "It's about time you called me. I was prepared to come to Atlanta. I don't have a clue what is going on."

Donald responded, " I was going to wait until I returned to Texas but I will be here for the next six weeks. When I returned I found out that my daughter's mother passed. She has been in foster care for the last six months. She was staying with one of the mother's of the church then Mother Florence became ill. She was moved to foster care. I thank God she was placed in a good home. Nancy has been through a lot. I do not want to transfer her until the end of the semester. I will be staying on post at Forest Park. I will be able to drive her to school and pick her up."

Catherine was quiet. She did not know how to respond. He had not asked her to come to Atlanta to meet his daughter, She worked in retail so she could not take off but he did not ask her to come to Atlanta. She needed to respond.

"Donald, I never knew you had a child. Were you married and divorced?"

Donald knew he owed her honesty. "Catherine, Theresa and I were never married. Theresa and I had no future together so she moved back to Atlanta. The last time I saw her was before I left for Iraq. I wanted to see my daughter. I don't know why but there was a sense of urgency. I took my parents pictures of her. I promised her I would give them her address so they could contact her. I never told Theresa that they moved to Washington. I never changed their address in the sysytem. My location was classified My daughter should never have been in foster care. I was irresponsible. As many times as I could have been blown up I never thought beyond myself. My father was angry with me because of how I had handled things after she was born. I was angry at him so I gave them the pictures and I left. My father said I will pray for you. Catherine, I am sorry that I was not honest with you. I'm sorry that you

Claudette Milner

found out this way. My first priority is my daughter. Before I can be in a relationship with anyone I have to learn to be a father."

"Donald. I could have taked custody of her until you retired"

"Catherine, we don't have a future. I have kept you on the fence because we compliment each other. I needed to be with you when I was home because of the pain I felt when I was away. Thank you for being in my life. After I retire from the military I don't know where I will live or what my future holds. Nancy lost her mother during the last year. She needs to know that I will not abandon her. This will be a transition for her. I am sorry. I am overwhelmed right now. I want to meet God's expectations of me."

Catherine did not want to cry so she said,

"God bless Donald and hung up."

As soon as she hung up the phone she began to cry. She thought she had finally met the man she was going to marry. She wanted to have his child before he retired. She had not been faithful but there was never any expectation from him that he expected fidelity. They kicked it when he was home. She knew this was not a love connection but she thought that he wanted it to be. She thought he was looking for a spouse to settle down with after his final tour of duty.

She really needed to stop trying to catch a military man. She wiped her tears and called Gary.

Donald received some paperwork fedx. He was going to pick up Nancy from Mrs. Heming's and spend some time with her. He dressed down and headed to Atlanta.

Nancy knew she was going to spend some time alone with her dad. Her grandparents Revrend Miller and his wife Maureen were nice. She knew she would be staying with them in Washinton but she did not know why she would not be staying with her father. She thought when he came to get her she would live with him. That is what she had been praying for. They had transferred her to AP classes so she was happier at Cromley. She had a new teacher. His name was Larry Lansing. He was a part of the Conoco field trip. She entered Mrs. Roberta's home. Mrs. Roberta asked her to change out of her uniform into some casual clothes.

"Nancy, what is the matter. I thought you would be happy to spend some time with your father."

"My grandparents left for Washington. I thought that I was going to leave with them. Is my daddy going to leave me to?"

"Nancy, there is papework that needed to be completed before your dad can have full custody. Your dad wanted you transferred into the STEM program so that you would enter school in Washington as a STEM student. You and your dad are going to live at the military base in Forrest Park until you finish the semester then you will move. I think that he was going to explain this to you but I see that you are upset."

They heard the doorbell. Mrs Roberta went to get the door. She asked if he could stay and answer Nancy's questions. I think she is afraid that you are going to go back to Texas without her."

Donald replied."Can I come in and we talk with her together. Being a father is new to me. The military now seems like a piece of cake."

Donald walked in and sat on the couch. He looked at his daughter. He saw a hint of sadness in her face. He wanted her face to show nothing but joy. He reached out and took her small hands into his.

"Nancy, the reason I am not taking you back to Texas is because my job with the military does not allow me to be a single parent with full custody. I have to go back overseas to Iraq for 6 months. That is why your grandparents will have custody until I retire. Write this date down. He gave her the date. I will retire from the Army on this date. Then you will be with me until you go away to college. I want you to finish the semester here in Atlanta. I received my final papers today. I will pick you up on Friday. The rooms are already furnished but you can decorate your bedroom. We have to buy some things like a broom and those things. I don't cook much but if you will help me I am sure we will not starve. You can take anything you want with you. We will buy some new clothes, a computer and anything else you need. I will be working at the base part time."

"How am I going to get to school?"

"I will take you and pick you up. Any other questions?

"Yes, Can I still go to church and Bible study at Mrs. Roberta's church."

"Yes, it has been a long time since I attended church."

"Do you believe in God?"

Donald had to think before he answered her question.

"I do now. He performed a maracle. He brought me home to you."

Roberta held back the tears and said. "You two better get going. She has homework to do."

"We will be back in a couple of hours. I'm sure my daughter has more questions for me.

Donald took his daughter to get some burgers. She had something in her coat pocket. She took it out and showed it to him. It was a picture of the two of them. He looked at it. He had never seen this picture. It was of the two of them right after she was born. Theresa had taken this picture when she came to give him the DNA results. She never said anything about having the picture.

Nancy said, "it was in the safety deposit box."

Then she took out a the same picture he had given to his parents except this one was of the two of them. It was if Theresa knew that without him she would be alone.

Nancy looked at her father and said. "I kept this picture and prayed every night. I had faith you would come and rescue me."

Donald did not care that he was in a public restaurant. He went over to his daughter gathered her in his arms and they cried together. Then they left hand in hand. He had walked away from the Lord many years ago. Despite it all. God had given him a second chance to make things right. God had blessed him with a new beginning.

Chapter 2
Love
Psalm 127:3

"Children are a blessing and a gift from the Lord."

Donald woke up early and prayed. Today was a day he needed his father to be there with him. He needed his dad to set him straight about parenthood. He called his father for instruction.

Rev. Miller simply told him. "There is a parenting book for instruction. It is the word of God. You can't watch it on youtube or google it. Your wisdom you will receive from God from the Holy Spirit. It is free to all that ask for it, There is no limit on minutes, no additional text charges and no voicemail and no information shared with your enemy. It is a private and confidential conversation with God. Once you are tapped into the source he will give you guidance, direction and instruction. God will be your source. He will be your partner in rearing your daughter. Your mother and I love you. Cherish everyday you have with Nancy until you ship out. This time you will understand that God has protected you all these years for this time. Can you come to our home for Thanksgiving. It will give us the opportunity to get to know her better."

Donald replied. "I will book our flights today. Thank you for agreeing to keep Nancy while I am on my final tour of duty. I love you."

Donald had not thought about Thanksgiving. He had not been home for a long time. His Thanksgiving meals had been spent in Iraq. It was just another day in the desert. He needed to introduce his family to his daughter.

Donald knelt in prayer just talking to God. He had left Nancy's room empty. He wanted her to fill it with her own things. He wanted it to be special to her. His parents had taken pictures while they were here. They would get frames for them. She needed to know that she had a family that loved her. She would never be alone again.

Donald entered Cromley Elementary and asked for the couselor Mrs. Simpson. He had called the day before and set the appointment. She came out to greet him. He was dressed in his military uniform.

Mrs. Simpson spoke first. "Sgt. Miller, thank you for your service. Please come back to my office so we can get all the paperwork completed."

Donald gave her his paperwork. For now he has permanent custody until he transfers her to the custody of his parents to make sure they are listed as her temporary guardian. Robin asked, "when are you moving to Washington?"

For the time being I will be staying in Forest Park at the military base until the end of the semester. Here is my current address. I will bring her to school and pick her up daily. It has been approved by the superintendant. Nancy has been through enough. She will not go through another transfer before we move. It is my expectation that all of the paperwork will be updated as soon as possible. When her records are transferred there are to be no flags on her account. My daughter will not be labeled by systemic racism. Are there any other forms you need from me?"

Mrs. Simpson hesitated then answered his question. "Sgt. Miller, will you be picking Nancy up today?"

"Yes, I will pick her up. Here is a copy of my ID. I have been informed that her new teacher is Larry Lansing. Is it possible for me to meet with him today?"

"He has a planning period in an hour and a half. I can call him and see if he is available.'

Mrs. Simpson called Mr. Lansing. He would love to meet with you Sgt. during his planning period.

Mrs. Simpson gave him back his ID. I will update the system.

"You will have to come back during Mr. Lansing's planning time."

Claudette Milner

"I am going to grab some lunch and I will return. Thank you for your assistance."

Donald knew that Nancy would be out of the school district so he put in for a hardship. He obtained the hardship so that Nancy would not have to change schools. He did not want to take Nancy to Washington until he had time to establish a relationship with her. He needed her to know that he was not going to just leave her with his parents. He was going to be a fulltime parent. He needed time to build her trust. There had been women in his life in Texas. He did not want her to know about his life in Texas. He did not want his previous relatinships to make her insecure about his commitment to her. Catherine had been calling wanting to be a mother figure for his daughter. This is what he was avoiding. Larry pulled into Sam's and ate lunch then he returned to the school to meet Mr. Lansing.

Donald checked in and waited for Larry to finish class. When Larry walked in Donald was surprised. He was not what he expected to see. He was an African American male MSAT intructor. There were less than five percent. He had stereotyped her teacher. He guessed he had to change his perspective also. He was not innocent of stereotyping. Larry shook his hand and led him back to his classroom. Larry pulled out Nancy's folder.

He and Donald had a regular parent teacher conference. Donald shared that Nancy would be transfering schools after the semester ended.

"Mr. Lansing, thank you for your support. I know this did not happen without your support. Thank you for not allowing these students to stay invisible."

Larry replied, "thank you. I wish all of our students had a happy ending. I did not accomplish this alone. I worked with the principal and the counselors. The need was brought to the attention of Ms. Steele, her teacher, when Nancy asked her why she could not go on the field trip to Conoco. She made an impact when she brought in a sample of the extra work she had been completing on a daily basis. Her efforts forced us to review the flagged students. It was your daughter that made this happen. She kept asking questions until we were forced to find solutions. She made her voice be heard. She is extremely intelligent. I am sure that with the grace of God she will achieve her goals.

Donald only had an hour before he would make a final trip to Mrs. Heming. He needed to shut that door as a residence. Roberta spent the morning washing all of Nancy's clothes and packing her things. She carefully packed her picture of her and her mother. She thought back to the time she agreed to receive Nancy. Being older she had decided to not accept any more placements. She had two that were sixteen years old, one 13 years old. The parents had relinquished parental rights. She hated seeing children transfer from one foster home to another. When they called her about Nancy she placed it in the hands of the Lord. There was something about this young lady. When they approved her although she was at her maximum if was her affirmation that this was where she was suppose to be. She was shy and quiet at first. Her mother had passed. One day she showed her a picture of her and her dad.

She said, "I am keeping this picture until God brings my father home to get me."

She looked at her and asked. "Where is your dad?"

"He's overseas. He came to see me before he left. He promised me he would come back to see me. The only thing I have is this picture of me and him. My mother is an angel. She is watching over us."

She asked, "does he have family?"

"No, he lives in Texas. His parents used to live in Colorado but I forget where they moved. He didn't have their new address. He said he was going to take a picture of me to them. I guess he forgot. Can you help me find them. My mother had a safety deposit box at the bank. Mother Florence has the key.

Roberta called the social worker and gave her all the information. She knew that Mother Florence had taken care of Nancy after her mother died. She stayed with her until she became ill. Nancy knew that her father's name was Sgt. Donald Miller. That was where the search began. God had interceded and now she was going home. She wanted to keep her until she left but God said no. She had to allow her father to become a man. She finished packing and took her things downstairs. The only thing left to do was praise God and give him the glory. She had baked a cake for the family so they could all say goodbye.

Donald rang the doorbell. Mrs. Roberta asked him if he would stay and have cake with them. He agreed. They took pictures and then began their new journey.

Donald decided they would stop and get sheets and a comforter for the bed. He had purchased towels and things for the bathroom. He had no clue about rearing a daughter. The only thing he could do was follow God's direction and call his mother. Tonight he would call his sisters. It was time..

Donald and Nancy spent hours in the store. She needed a lamp and other things for her room. They picked up two pieces and went back to the base to get her settled in to her room. They prayed then she went sound asleep.

Claudette Milner

He called his parents and obtained his sisters numbers. They would be in Washington for Thanksgiving.

Forgiven of Our Transgressions: Nancy Deming, Faith

Chapter 3
Family
1 Corinthians 13: 4-8

"Love is patient, love is kind. It does not envy, it does not boast, it is not proud. It does not dishonor others, it is not self-seeking, it is not easily angered, it keeps no record of wrongs. Love does not delight in evil but rejoices with the truth. It always protects, always trusts, always hopes, always perseveres. Love never fails."

Donald spoke to both of his sisters. He knew that his parents have already shared the news with them. Katie was kind and understanding. She received the information in love. Beatrice yelled and yelled at his irresponsibility. He allowed her to vent then he got off the phone.

He heard the cell phone ring. He recognized the number. He started not to pick up the phone, but he knew he had to resolve the issue.

He picked up the phone prepared for a tongue lashing. Before he could say anything, Beatrice began to speak.

"I am sorry. I am so hurt that you kept this from me. You are my little brother. You could have been killed overseas. I may have never known that I had a niece. Momma filled in the gapes for me. They had to tell us because we kept asking them why they were in Atlanta. Why didn't you call me Donald? Why didn't you call me? I want to be a part of your life. I want to be a part of her life. Please just don't shut the family out."

"Bea, I'm sorry. One day I was single and free. The next day I found out my daughter was in foster care. I did not have time to update the family. I have been in parent mode. Theresa always took care of Nancy. I depended on her to make sure she was safe and cared for. I lived my life to fit my needs. I never thought of her when I kept signing up for additional tours of duty. I never thought that Theresa would die. The only thing I think about now is making sure my daughter is safe. I want Nancy to know the family. Her grandparents are dead. We are the only family that she has. We will be home for Thanksgiving."

Bea stopped then began to speak. "I am moving to Tacoma after Christmas with my family. I would like to be there to help with Nancy while you are overseas. Can I ask why you are staying in Atlanta instead of with our parents.?

He knew she needed the truth. "The last time I saw Nancy was right before I was deployed. I promised her I would come back. She needs to know that I am her father. I am not going to walk out on her or abandon her. I needed private time with her to build her trust. I want her to be respectful to mom and dad but as grandparents. Dad needed to know that I am going to take full responsibility for my daughter. Bea, I grew up these last couple of months. God stopped me in my tracks. I love you. Thank you for being there for my daughter."

"You can call me anytime Donald. You can duo me so she can meet the boys. Demetrius is her age. I have been looking at private schools in the area. I will send you the information I have. There are two excellent magnet schools which have good AP programs. I will send that to you also. What are her interest?"

"Bea, she wants to be an astronaut. Can you believe my daughter wants to be an astronaut. Thank you for not beating me up again. I love you."

Bea turned to her husband Christian.

"I know, thank you for being my husband. This family is going to be there for my brother and his daughter. Thank you for supporting me in this move."

Christian replied. "You have always supported me now it's time for me to support you. I want you to soar. You have made concessions in your career for our family. Your parents are getting older. This is a great move for us. I am going to continue to work remote. During the pandemic companies had to reinvent themselves. The ability to work remote prevents transfers every time you get promoted. It keeps family more cohesive. You will be Chief of Staff at the hospital. We are proud of you Dr. Beatrice Monroe."

"I love you Christian Monroe."

It took a minute for Donald to get with the schedule. He took Nancy to the hairdresser and had them braid her hair. He realized after a couple of days at school she needed a computer now. He read all the recommendations and they went and bought one. She also needed a printer and a desk. He connected with both his sisters at least once a week. Today was Wednesday night they attended Bible study together. He had returned to his roots. Every time he meditated, he received new information from God. Every time he looked in his daughters eyes, he knew she missed her mom. When they moved to Washington, he would have her things shipped to his parents.

Nancy had been staying over on Wednesday nights for choir practice. Sunday, they had to be at church early because they were singing. Nancy took the microphone from the choir director and led them in Sweet Hour of Prayer, her mother's favorite song. At the end he walked forward and hugged her. After church Mrs. Roberta hugged her.

Before they left, they talked. Larry advised her that they were going to spend Thanksgiving in Washington with his parents. He thanked her for the invitation.

Nancy woke up the next night crying. I dreamed that my mother finally transcended to Heaven. I am not crying because I miss her. I am crying because now I know that everything is going to be ok. She will now be at peace. I know I need to wait until I am settled to be baptized but I want to be baptized now. I want to accept Jesus as my savior. I want the Holy Spirit to live in me. I hear you pray at night. I hear you speaking directly with God. I want that kind of relationship with him."

"Nancy, my father is a minister. Will you speak with him when we arrive in Tacoma for Thanksgiving."

Nancy asked. Why didn't you tell me that. I was wondering who was going to take me to church."

Donald laughed. I can guarantee you that is not something you have to worry about.

Nancy arrived at school ten minutes early. She was excited because she was going to get to see the three women engineers from Conoco. They were recruiting for the Stem Club. Although she was moving, she wanted to hear all the information. Maybe they would have a club in Washington.

The guest were Miya Wong Tidwell II, Jean Brown, and Juanita Stewart.

Jean asked if anyone had any questions.

Karen raised her hand. "I am moving to Tacoma Washington. Do they have any aerospace companies that have Stem Clubs?"

Miya answered her question. There are STEM programs in that area. I will see if I can reach out to one of our conference speakers and send the information to Mr. Lansing.

After they left Larry advised the male students that Conoco was in the process of starting a STEM club for boys. They would have the information available before the break.

Nancy was looking forward to the break when she would meet the rest of the family. Everyday that she got up she thanked God for her blessings.

Donald and Nancy packed one suitcase of luggage each for their trip. Rev. Miller picked them up at the Airport. They lived thirty minutes from the airport. He and Nancy talked all the way home. She was asking him about baptism. He turned to Donald.

"I was expecting a lot of questions but not about baptism and the Holy Spirit. Nancy, today after dinner we will spend time discussing salvation and the receiving of the

Holy Spirit. I don't want to rush it because this is the most important day of your life when you take God as your heavenly father.

Maureen ran outside when her husband drove into the driveway. This was the fulfillment of her prayers. She hugged her granddaughter and took her things to her room. It had been a long time since her son had stayed at the house. She asked Nancy if she wanted to help her make some Banana Pudding? She showed her to the bathroom so she could wash her hands then led her to the kitchen. She knew that Maureen and Katie would be in tonight. She thanked God again.

After dinner Rev. Miller and Nancy went into the den to talk.

He began," Nancy I sense an urgency about wanting to be baptized."

"My mother did not accept Christ as her savior until after she had me. She went into the hospital with Covid 19 and never came out. What if she had never accepted Christ as her savior? I would never see her again. I don't know what will happen tomorrow. I want to be prepared in case Jesus comes. Grandpa, I don't want to wonder about where I will spend my eternal life. I want the assurance of my home."

"Nancy, if your father does not object. I will baptize you on Sunday morning. I will speak to him tonight."

He hugged his granddaughter. Your aunts and their families are here. I will take you to the family room to meet him. Please ask your father to come in to speak with me.

Donald came in and his father shut the door. He looked at Donald.

"I know we have had many disagreements but the one thing I know for sure is that Nancy is ready to be baptized. She understands the meaning of salvation. I would like to baptize her on Sunday."

"Dad, I would ask only one thing of you."

"What is that Donald?"

"That you allow me to rededicate my life to Christ."

"Donald, this will be the fulfillment of my prayers. I will keep this undern wraps until Thanksgiving Day. We have so much to be thankful for."

Donald found Nancy in the midst of cousins and family. The ladies were finishing up in the kitchen making homemade baked goods.

Donald waited until everyone left to speak to his daughter. After they said their prayers and he tucked her in he gave her the news.

"Nancy, your grandfather will baptize you on Sunday. I am going to rededicate my life to God."

Nancy hugged her father and went to sleep in a place of peace.

Thanksgiving Day began with a service of Praise at the Friendship Memorial Baptist Church. Afterward the family met at their parents house and celebrated the Lord.

Christian sat down at the piano and accompanied Nancy as she sang Sweet Hour of Prayer. He followed up with Amazing Grace.

During the meal Donald announced the baptism and rededication. His mother cried. On Friday Nancy went with her grandmother and her aunts to shop while the men stayed glued to the television watching football.

Larry took a break and went to the study.

Christian joined him "I thought you might need to talk."

"Thank you, everything happened so fast that I have not had time to catch my breath. I needed this time with the family. I needed to know that Nancy would be okay while I am away. I needed to know she would never end up in foster care again."

"I don't know what your plans are after you retire but there are good schools and growing businesses here in Tacoma. Whatever your decision I am your brother -in -law but I will always be here to talk with or help you with the challenges of single parenthood."

Donald replied, "Christian, I owe you one. Thank you for calming my sister down. I will always think of you as my brother."

Donald laughed. "We better get back to the game before Daddy puts us to work on that shed."

Sunday morning was a special day for the Miller family. That morning after church before they began the baptismal service Rev. Miller opened the doors of the church. Sgt. Donald Miller stood before the church to rededicate his life to Christ. The family came up and prayed with him. Thirty minutes later he sat on the front pew and cried as he saw his daughter baptized. There was no greater gift than seeing his child accept Christ as her savior. Now he knew no matter what the future held. She would never be alone.

Forgiven of Our Transgressions: Nancy Deming, Faith

About the Series
Author Claudette Milner

The Forgiven of Our Transgressions Series begins with Forgiven of Our Transgressions Psalm 32:1 The series includes 51 Editions and is based in Atlanta GA. It discusses the complexities of today's society and the mission of the church when ministering to the world. It focuses on the seeking of wisdom and guidance from God while exemplifying mercy, compassion, and grace to all mankind. It asks the question throughout. Where would I be in my life if it was guided by God. This is the 51st edition entitled Forgiven of Our Transgressions: Nancy Deming, Faith

Claudette Milner

,

About the Author

Claudette Milner is the author of the Forgiven of Our Transgressions series. Editions 1-51
She is also the author of the Children of Plains Estates series which includes Volumes 1-5
Her novelettes include It Started with a Dime: Malachi 3:10, Mary: Jerimiah 1:5. Journey to the Cross
Her first poetry book is We Give You Praise: Thoughts from the Holy Spirit and MP3 We Give You Praise.
Workbooks Include: Are You Walking in the Spirit or Walking in the Flesh? and The Rejuvenation of the Church: Meeting the Needs of Our Youth Guide and Workbook

CONTACT US

Contact me for book signings, workshops, song writing, and motivational speaking

Email: claudette.milner@gmail,com

Facebook: https://www.facebook.com/claudettemilnerauthor

LinkedIn https://www.linkedin.com/in/claudette-milner-5771071b/

https://www.amazon.com/Claudette-Milner/e/B003BME2XU%3Fref=dbs_a_mng_rwt_scns_share

www.claudettemilner.com

twitter: claudettemilner1

Made in the USA
Columbia, SC
23 November 2022

Claudette Milner